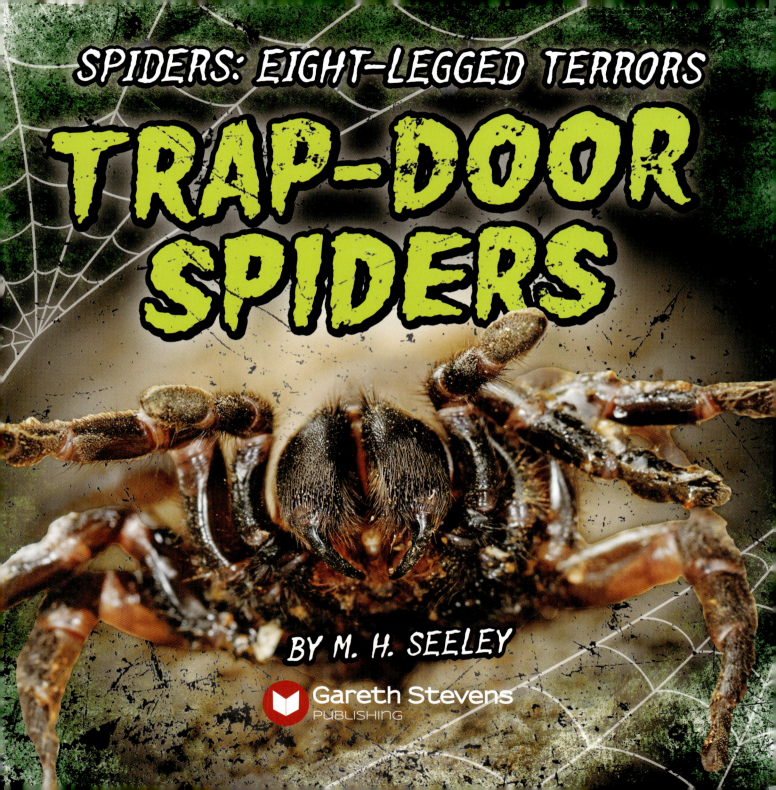

Please visit our website, www.garethstevens.com. For a free color catalog of all our high-quality books, call toll free 1-800-542-2595 or fax 1-877-542-2596.

Cataloging-in-Publication Data

Names: Seeley, M. H.
Title: Trap-door spiders / M. H. Seeley.
Description: New York : Gareth Stevens Publishing, 2018. | Series: Spiders: eight-legged terrors | Includes index.
Identifiers: ISBN 9781538202135 (pbk.) | ISBN 9781538202159 (library bound) | ISBN 9781538202142 (6 pack)
Subjects: LCSH: Trap-door spiders–Juvenile literature.
Classification: LCC QL458.4 S4535 2018 | DDC 595.4'4–dc23

First Edition

Published in 2018 by
Gareth Stevens Publishing
111 East 14th Street, Suite 349
New York, NY 10003

Copyright © 2018 Gareth Stevens Publishing

Designer: Laura Bowen
Editor: Ryan Nagelhout

Photo credits: Cover, p. 1 (spider) Matteo photos/Shutterstock.com; cover, pp. 1–24 (background) Fantom666/Shutterstock.com; cover, pp. 1–24 (black splatter) Miloje/Shutterstock.com; cover, pp. 1–24 (web) Ramona Kaulitzki/Shutterstock.com; pp. 4–24 (text boxes) Tueris/Shutterstock.com; p. 5 Auscape/UIG/Getty Images; p. 7 Animalparty/Wikimedia Commons; p. 9 James H Robinson/Getty Images; p. 11 Bucky Reeves/Getty Images; p. 13 DR PAUL ZAHL/Getty Images; p. 15 Simon D Pollard/Getty Images; p. 17 photo by Alan Cressler/Getty Images; p. 19 Steve Kaufman/Getty Images; p. 21 Nicolas LE CORRE/Gamma-Rapho/Getty Images.

All rights reserved. No part of this book may be reproduced in any form without permission in writing from the publisher, except by a reviewer.

Printed in China

CPSIA compliance information: Batch #CS17GS: For further information contact Gareth Stevens, New York, New York at 1-800-542-2595.

CONTENTS

Hide-and-Seek 4

All in the Family 6

Night Hunting 8

Love on Eight Legs 10

No Place Like Home 12

Please Don't Bite 14

Shovel Teeth 16

Friends and Enemies 18

Sharing the Planet 20

Glossary 22

For More Information 23

Index 24

Words in the glossary appear in **bold** type the first time they are used in the text.

HIDE-AND-SEEK

You won't find trap-door spiders around your house or hanging from tree branches. You won't find their webs in untouched corners of the bookshelf. In fact, you won't find their webs at all. The trap-door spider, unlike many of its kind, doesn't make a web.

Instead, these creatures live in **burrows** underground, usually hidden by a door covered with dirt and plant matter. The door is hung on one side using silk the spider produces. Silk lines reach out around the burrow entrance as a kind of alarm system.

TERRIFYING TRUTHS

Certain types of wasps are known to sting trap-door spiders, take them back to their nest, and lay eggs on their body so their babies have a fresh source of food!

The trap-door spider hides its burrow entrance with a door that blends in with the ground around it.

ALL IN THE FAMILY

Several different spider families have trap-door spiders. In the *Liphistius* genus alone there are 50 species, or kinds, of trap-door spider. Each has special habits and ways of building their burrow. Some types of trap-door spiders are more common than others, but most are found where it's warm.

Though each species is different, they all use their trap-door to catch **prey** and hide from predators. They're mostly **nocturnal** and catch food by hiding in their burrow until prey passes by.

TERRIFYING TRUTHS

A recently discovered species of trap-door spider, the *Aptostichus barackobamai*, is named for former US president Barack Obama!

A TRAP-DOOR SPIDER'S BURROW

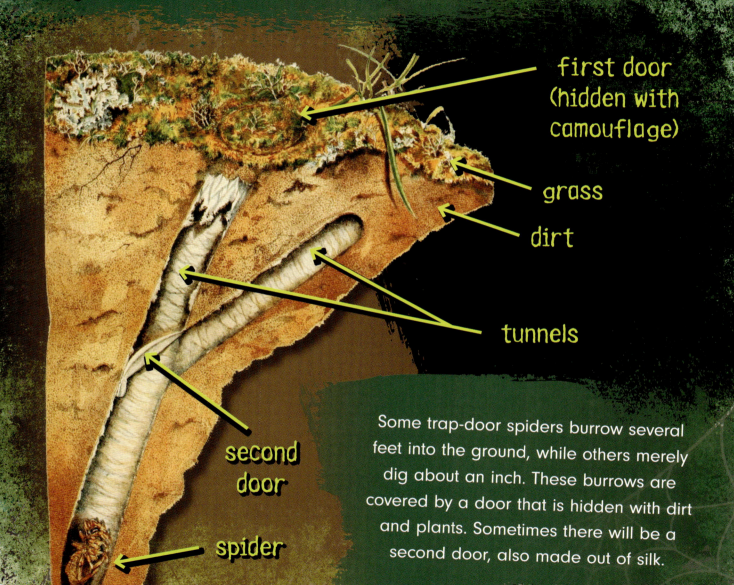

first door (hidden with camouflage)
grass
dirt
tunnels
second door
spider

Some trap-door spiders burrow several feet into the ground, while others merely dig about an inch. These burrows are covered by a door that is hidden with dirt and plants. Sometimes there will be a second door, also made out of silk.

NIGHT HUNTING

Trap-door spiders sleep during the day and eat during the night, when their prey least expects it. They lay lines of silk out from the door and wait for something to wander by. The silk **vibrates** as it's walked on, and the vibrations help the spider figure out how big and how close the creature is.

If they sense that it's the right size for eating, trap-door spiders will throw open the door, bite the prey, and drag it into the burrow to eat for dinner.

TERRIFYING TRUTHS

Trap-door spiders aren't picky. They'll eat all kinds of bugs, frogs, baby birds and baby snakes, mice, small fish, and even other spiders!

A trap-door spider hides behind its door until it's ready to strike.

LOVE ON EIGHT LEGS

Trap-door spiders can live up to 20 years. Females generally live longer than males because males must leave their burrow to find a female to make babies with—no easy job when all the females are in hiding!

When a male finds a burrow, he must be very careful when he goes knocking—if the female thinks he's a predator, she won't let him in. And if she thinks he's prey, she might eat him! In fact, she might eat him anyway!

TERRIFYING TRUTHS

Baby trap-door spiders, called spiderlings, live with their mother for several months before going to dig their own burrows.

male trap-door spider

A female trap-door spider might eat a male after **mating** or if she doesn't want him as a partner.

11

NO PLACE LIKE HOME

Because there are so many kinds of trap-door spiders, they can be found in many different places around the world. Usually, trap-door spiders like to live where it's warm, because the ground is soft enough to dig their burrows. They're often found in Australia, Asia, Africa, South America, and North America—especially the warmer parts of North America, like the Southeast and West.

Though these spiders may live in your area, you may never see one, because they're so often hiding in their burrow. Trap-door spiders are famously shy!

TERRIFYING TRUTHS

Brown trap-door spiders, a common species, are often mistaken for funnel-web spiders—one of the deadliest spiders in the world!

This trap-door spider's burrow only has one door. It's right at surface level so the spider can snatch up prey that's just walking on the ground.

13

PLEASE DON'T BITE

Most species of trap-door spiders are nonaggressive, which means that they don't like fighting. Though they look scary—with two large **fangs** they use to bring in their prey—most trap-door spiders just want to be left alone.

Most species of trap-door spiders have a bite that's not toxic to humans. The area around a trap-door spider bite will hurt a lot and probably swell up, but there won't be any lasting harm. Still, if a trap-door spider bites you, it's best to go see a doctor. Better safe than sorry!

TERRIFYING TRUTHS

Scientists think they may be able to use trap-door spider **venom** to make pesticides, which are mixtures used to kill bugs.

Trap-door spiders have two large fangs they use to bite prey and fill them with venom.

SHOVEL TEETH

Trap-door spiders' bodies are designed to help them survive. Their jaws are different from some other types of spiders because they have sharp bumps along their jaw that act like teeth. But trap-door spiders don't use these teeth for chewing food—they use them for chewing dirt when they're digging their burrow!

Trap-door spiders also have two large fangs that they use to capture their prey. Some species have extra mouthparts called "pedipalps" (PEH-duh-palps). Pedipalps help with digging, shaping silk for burrow building, and eating.

TERRIFYING TRUTHS

Some trap-door spiders have fangs as long as 1 cm—that's almost half an inch!

pedipalps

Pedipalps look a bit like a fifth pair of legs.

FRIENDS AND ENEMIES

Trap-door spiders aren't picky about what they eat, which makes them good for people's gardens because they'll eat a lot of the bugs that can harm plants. But the world is a dangerous place for these creatures.

Scorpions and centipedes will eat trap-door spiders. The spiders are also prey for birds, raccoons, skunks, and an Australian animal called a bandicoot. No wonder these little guys like to stay safe at home—it's no fun for the predator when it becomes prey!

TERRIFYING TRUTHS

Though trap-door spiders look tough and mean to humans, they're great for pest control.

Trap-door spiders enjoy being predators, but when animals like the bandicoot are hungry, they can easily become prey!

SHARING THE PLANET

Trap-door spiders are in danger of **extinction** when their habitat, or where they live, is destroyed. One species, the Kanthan Cave trap-door spider, is on the **endangered** species list. This spider makes its home in a single cave in Malaysia, which may be harmed as a result of human use.

Although spiders often look scary, remember that they're an important part of keeping nature healthy. We need to keep their homes in place so they can help us keep our gardens free of bugs!

TERRIFYING TRUTHS

People who keep trap-door spiders as pets can get bitten because the spider mistakes their hand for prey.

Only experts and experienced spider handlers should handle trap-door spiders. It's best to leave them in their burrow!

GLOSSARY

burrow: a hole in the ground made by an animal, or to make a hole in the ground

endangered: at risk of dying out

extinction: when a species of something dies out completely

fang: a hard, sharp-pointed body part a spider uses to put venom in its prey

mate: to come together to make babies

nocturnal: active at night

prey: an animal hunted by other animals for food

venom: poison created by one animal to harm another

vibrate: to move back and forth quickly

FOR MORE INFORMATION

BOOKS

Britton, Tamara L. *Trapdoor Spiders*. Edina, MN: ABDO Publishing, 2011.

Goldish, Meish. *Tricky Trapdoor Spiders*. New York, NY: Bearport Publishing, 2009.

Kolpin, Molly. *Trapdoor Spiders*. Mankato, MN: Capstone Press, 2011.

WEBSITES

Trap-Door Spider
animalcorner.co.uk/animals/trapdoor-spider
Learn more about the habitat, diet, and lives of trap-door spiders.

Trap-Door Spider
sciencechannel.com/tv-shows/monster-bug-wars/videos/monster-bug-wars-trapdoor-spider
Watch a video about the trap-door spider and see how it catches its prey.

What's Hiding Behind the Trapdoor?
sciencedaily.com/releases/2016/08/160830101211.htm
Learn about a newly discovered species of trap-door spider in Australia.

Publisher's note to educators and parents: Our editors have carefully reviewed these websites to ensure that they are suitable for students. Many websites change frequently, however, and we cannot guarantee that a site's future contents will continue to meet our high standards of quality and educational value. Be advised that students should be closely supervised whenever they access the Internet.

INDEX

Africa 12
Asia 12
Australia 12
babies 10
burrows 4, 5, 6, 7, 8, 10, 12, 13, 16, 21
door 4, 5, 7, 9, 13
endangered species 20
extinction 20
fangs 14, 15, 16
females 10, 11
habitat 20
jaws 16
males 10, 11
North America 12
pedipalps 16, 17
pets 20
predators 6, 10, 18, 19
prey 6, 8, 10, 13, 15, 16, 18, 19, 20
silk 4, 7, 8, 16
South America 12
species 6, 12, 14, 20
spiderlings 10
teeth 16
venom 14, 15